CELEBRATE THE UNITED STATES!

WHY DO WE SAY THE PLEDGE OF ALLEGIANCE?

BY BEATRICE HARRIS

Gareth Stevens PUBLISHING

Please visit our website, www.garethstevens.com. For a free color catalog of all our high-quality books, call toll free 1-800-542-2595 or fax 1-877-542-2596.

Library of Congress Cataloging-in-Publication Data
Names: Harris, Beatrice, author.
Title: Why do we say the Pledge of Allegiance? / Beatrice Harris.
Description: New York : Gareth Stevens Publishing, 2026. | Series: Celebrate the United States! | Includes index.
Identifiers: LCCN 2024059874 (print) | LCCN 2024059875 (ebook) | ISBN 9781482471120 (library binding) | ISBN 9781482471113 (paperback) | ISBN 9781482471137 (ebook)
Subjects: LCSH: Bellamy, Francis. Pledge of Allegiance to the Flag–Juvenile literature. | Flags–Law and legislation–United States–Juvenile literature.
Classification: LCC JC346 .B453 2026 (print) | LCC JC346 (ebook) | DDC 323.6/50973–dc23/eng/20250220
LC record available at https://lccn.loc.gov/2024059874
LC ebook record available at https://lccn.loc.gov/2024059875

Published in 2026 by
Gareth Stevens Publishing
2544 Clinton Street
Buffalo, NY 14224

Designer: Jeffrey Taylor
Editor: Therese Shea

Photo credits: Series art (blue background) Paladin12/Shutterstock.com; Cover, p. 1 Jihan Nafiaa Zahri/Shutterstock.com; p. 5 AI Generated/Shutterstock.com; p. 7 Joseph Sohm/Shutterstock.com; p. 8 (inset) Unknown photographer/commons.wikimedia.org; p. 9 Willis & Rand/commons.wikimedia.org.com; p. 11 Limolida Design Studio/Shutterstock.com; p. 13 AI Generated/Shutterstock.com; p. 15 AI Generated/Shutterstock.com; p. 17 Dennis MacDonald/Shutterstock.com; p. 19 Jonathan Weiss/Alamy.com; p. 21 AI Generated/Shutterstock.com.

Printed in the United States of America

Some of the images in this book illustrate individuals who are models. The depictions do not imply actual situations or events.

CPSIA compliance information: Batch #CS26GS: For further information contact Gareth Stevens at 1-800-542-2595.

CONTENTS

Boldface words appear in the glossary.

"I Pledge Allegiance . . ."

Do you say the Pledge of Allegiance at school? Millions of children in American schools do, every school day. Adults say it too. Did you ever wonder why? Let's learn more about this pledge and what it means!

It's a Promise

Let's start with the name: the Pledge of Allegiance. A pledge is a promise. Allegiance means **loyalty**. By saying this pledge, you're promising, in front of the flag, to be loyal and respectful to the United States, which is called the **Republic**.

A Short History

Francis Bellamy wrote the first **version** of the pledge that is said today. It was printed in a **magazine** for young people called *Youth's Companion* in 1892. The pledge was meant to help young people feel **patriotism** for the United States.

Francis Bellamy

YOUTH'S COMPANION.

Published Weekly, by Willis & Rand, at the Office of the Boston Recorder, No. 127, Washington-Street.... Price One Dollar a year in advance, or $1,50, if not paid in advance

No. 33. | BOSTON, JANUARY 5, 1831. | Vol. IV.

THE LIBRARY.

THE EVIL OF THEFT.

The above engraving is the frontispiece to an admirable little work, written by the author of the Family Temperance Meeting, entitled "The Evil of Theft: exhibited in the History of James Forest, a penitent Sabbath Scholar."—Published by James Loring, No. 132, Washington-Street.

It is our earnest desire that the young readers of the Youth's Companion and all others who enjoy the delightful privilege of belonging to "the precious Sabbath School," will always hearken to the counsels and admonitions of the beloved Sabbath School teachers, and thus be secure from such evil conduct as was for a time pursued by the lad, an extract from whose history is now given. We wish our little readers to be sensible that their teachers feel great interest in their welfare. Whilst this boy was universally despised, his Sabbath School Teacher visited him and was the means of his reformation.

The news soon spread through the town, that James Forrest had been sent to jail for stealing. Among others, Mr. Howard heard of it, and it grieved him to the heart. That any child should be so wicked would have pained him; but that one who had attended the Sabbath School, and promised well for a season, should have fallen so sadly, affected him very deeply.

The prison where James was sent, was about five miles from Mr. Howard's residence; and as soon as he could make arrangements for leaving his business, taking a Bible with him, he set off to visit this unhappy boy. As the keeper of the prison was acquainted with Mr. Howard's character, he had no difficulty in obtaining admittance. He found James in a miserable situation; he was lying, pale and exhausted on his pallet, his allowance of food standing by him, untasted. His countenance at first brightened, on seeing Mr. Howard, for he knew him to be a true friend; but he instantly covered his face, and burst into tears. Mr. Howard was not ashamed to weep at a scene like this; his tears mingled with the boy's, and for a moment he was silent. He then said,

"O James, I did not expect to see you here." Receiving no reply, he proceeded,

"I see, my poor boy, that you have suffered much, and that you are now very unhappy: but remember, James, that all this misery is in consequence of sin. Had you continued at the Sabbath School, and hearkened to the instructions you received there, your situation would now have been very different. You might have become humble and penitent; have left off all your wicked ways; have been daily growing in grace and in the knowledge of our Lord and Savior,—happy yourself, and a blessing to your friends. But instead of this, you first slighted instruction, and then refused it altogether; you associated with bad company, and indulged your evil inclinations without restraint;—and you see, James, to what they have brought you. You have engaged in the service of Satan, and you find him a hard master; he pays his servants with much sorrow in this life, and with greater misery hereafter. In keeping the Lord's commandments, 'there is great reward,' but 'the wages of sin is death.' You have tasted but little of the misery which will follow a life of sin; but you have found the beginning of it bitter. Be warned, then, I entreat you, to 'forsake the path of the wicked, to turn from it and live.'"

The boy continued to weep, but made no reply, and Mr. Howard proceeded,

"I do not wish, James, to reproach you, nor to add unnecessarily to the pain you feel; but I do wish to convince you of your sin; I wish you to loathe it, and to feel that it is an *evil thing and bitter*, that you have sinned against the Lord,—that you have rejected all the offers of His mercy, and chosen to disobey His commandments. Your guilt is very great; and I cannot—I dare not—administer consolation, till I see you deeply sensible of it, and anxious to be delivered from sin, as well as suffering. The Lord Jesus Christ came into the world to die for sinners; but it is only penitent sinners who are saved. All who truly believe in him, repent of sin, and forsake it. Do you wish me to pray that you may be of this number?"

James faintly said, "Yes sir."

Mr Howard kneeled, and most fervently implored the divine mercy in behalf of this poor boy. He *felt* deeply for him, and this imparted an earnestness to his petitions, which affected James very much. Some feelings of real penitence appeared to be excited in his bosom; and when Mr. Howard rose from his knees, James asked him to tell him about "the thief on the cross." Mr. Howard read this, and several other passages from the Bible, and tried to explain them to the comprehension of James. He then urged him to take some food, and to encourage him to do so, himself tasted of the coarse, but wholesome provision, which was allowed the prisoner.

When James became sufficiently calm to converse, he made a full and free confession of his guilt, and expressed great sorrow that he had ever left the school. Among other circumstances, he mentioned his stealing the pencil from Mr. Thomson, and said he always felt unhappy at school after that.

He was much grieved to learn that Mr. Thomson remained very sick.

Mr. Howard told him that, should he hear of one of his scholars being in prison for theft, he feared, in his present weak state, it might prove too much for him.

James wept afresh at this, and begged that Mr. Howard would tell him he was sorry for his sin, and hoped he should never steal again.

"Do you feel," said Mr. Howard, "that it is right for you to be separated from all your friends, and punished by imprisonment?"

James promptly replied, that it was right.

"Have you felt unkindly towards the magistrate who condemned you?" asked Mr. Howard.

"I thought, at first, he might pardon me; but I feel now that he was right."

"Had you rather remain here, or go out and steal again, if you could avoid detection?"

"It is bad staying here, but I have not felt worse than I did the night after I took the money."

"If the Lord spares your life and permits you to return home, shall you feel angry with Mr. Martyn for sending you here?"

"I do not feel angry with him now; and I love Mrs. Martyn; she is very kind."

Having conversed with James as much as he thought would be profitable at once, and the jailer having come to let him out, for he had been locked into the room, Mr. Howard prepared to go. James begged him to stay longer, and clung to him as if he were his only friend. Mr. Howard gently disengaged himself, and leaving his Bible, in which he had marked several passages for James to read, he bade him good-bye, promising to come again as soon as he could.

"Remember, James," he said, "that the Lord is ever present with you, that it is against Him you have sinned, and that He will permit you at all times to approach Him to confess your sin, and to ask His mercy. 'God be merciful to me a sinner,' is the most proper petition for you, and I hope you will offer it from a broken and contrite heart."

Mr. Howard's engagements were such, that it was several days before he could again seek admittance to the prison.

NARRATIVE.

THE ELDER.

I learned, from early youth, to look upon the face of the Village Elder, with a mingled feeling of delight and awe; of delight, because of the placid and unchanging sweetness of composure that always sat upon his countenance, and broke into a smile whenever he spoke; and of awe, because of the presence of a holy man, one who served God daily, and who, next to the minister, dealt out to the little church the bread that never perisheth. I remember when first he came to my father's house and called us around him, patted our flaxen heads, and asked us about Christ and the Bible, that I feared to speak in his presence. But as I approached a period more mature, and heard, in circles where the name of Him in heaven was blasphemed, and from those who spent the sacred sabbath in revelry, and pointed the despising finger at all that was sacred in religion, the aged elder's name mocked at and turned to ridicule; and, marked with how much bitterness of hatred and malignity of heart, they spoke of him who they confessed had never injured them—and when I saw the good all united to him in love and confidence, my fear turned into admiration, and the hostility of others sealed my affection towards him forever.

Meeting from him in all our now frequent intercourse a father's tenderness, it was right that he should share, as he did, in much of that confidence and esteem which youthful minds naturally bestow on parental worth; and I was long anxious to know the reason, why so much of virtue in a harmless old man, should create enmity in any bosom.—In the early kindlings of juvenile thought, I fancied all would love goodness wherever they saw it even for its very sake. I saw the contrary, but it was a problem I could not solve.

One afternoon in August, just at the clearing up of a racking thunder storm, and while the rainbow that succeeded it spanned the valley with its beauteous hues, I was sent on an important errand to one of the farm houses on the oak meadows, the residence of De Otto, a man who I well recollected often to have heard dealing out the most bitter curses against the aged servant of the sanctuary. This circumstance was brought to mind by a singular incident that day. When I had reached the first of the creeks which run between the village and

Some of the pledge's words have changed or been added over the years. The pledge we say is from 1954. These are the words:

"I pledge allegiance to the Flag of the United States of America, and to the Republic for which it stands, one Nation under God, indivisible, with liberty and justice for all."

Pledge of Allegiance Word Review

word	what it means
pledge	promise
allegiance	loyalty
indivisible	unable to be taken apart
liberty	freedom
justice	fair treatment

Part of the Code

The United States has a flag **code**. It says how Americans should act toward the U.S. flag and care for it. The flag code is part of the law but isn't mandatory, or required. The Pledge of Allegiance became part of the flag code in 1942.

Not Just Talking

The flag code says people should recite, or say, the Pledge of Allegiance in a certain way to show respect. First, they stand if they can. Then, they face the flag. Next, they place their right hand over their heart. Finally, they recite the pledge.

More Rules

The flag code says men should take off hats or other **nonreligious** head coverings before they recite the pledge. They should hold them with their right hand at their left shoulder. People in **military** uniforms should not remove their hats. They should be silent, face the flag, and may do a **salute**.

When It's Said

Besides at many schools, where is the Pledge of Allegiance recited? It's also said at the beginning of the workday in U.S. Congress. Some state and local governments also recite the pledge before starting the business of the day.

Indiana House
of
Representatives
Monday, January 9, 2023
EXIT
SEAL OF THE STATE OF INDIANA
1816

Another Right

American citizens have many rights and freedoms. The U.S. **Supreme Court** said in 1943 that no one has to say the pledge. They have the right not to. But for many, saying the pledge is a way of showing respect for their country each day.

GLOSSARY

code: A set of rules or laws on how to behave or do things.

loyalty: Being faithful or supportive.

magazine: A type of printed material that is published every week or month.

military: The armed forces.

nonreligious: Not having to do with religion, or a way of honoring a god or gods.

patriotism: Love for one's country.

republic: A form of government in which the people elect, or choose by voting, representatives who run the government.

salute: To perform a sign of respect, such as raising the right hand to the side of the head.

Supreme Court: The highest court in the United States.

version: A form of something that is different from others.

FOR MORE INFORMATION

BOOKS

Earley, Christina. *Pledge of Allegiance*. New York, NY: Crabtree Publishing Company, 2023.

Taylor, Charlotte. *The Truth About U.S. Symbols*. New York, NY: Enslow Publishing, 2023.

WEBSITES

Pledge of Allegiance 1892
bensguide.gpo.gov/j-pledge-allegiance
Check out a review of how the Pledge of Allegiance came to be.

The Pledge of Allegiance
www.ushistory.org/documents/pledge.htm
Find out how the words of the pledge have changed over the years.

Publisher's note to educators and parents: Our editors have carefully reviewed these websites to ensure that they are suitable for students. Many websites change frequently, however, and we cannot guarantee that a site's future contents will continue to meet our high standards of quality and educational value. Be advised that students should be closely supervised whenever they access the internet.

INDEX